What People
The Law of At

Christopher's message is that, by using the Law of Attraction, you can achieve the discipline of positive thinking. Thus, there is no limit to what you can be, do or have! This book is a must-read for any teen wanting to better direct the course of his or her own life.

— Michael J. Losier,
author, *Law of Attraction*

The author's message that "what you think about, you bring about" shows the importance of learning to manage your emotions, so that you can get the results you want. Believe that you can do it!

— Jennifer L. Youngs,
co-author of the best-seller,
Taste Berries for Teens: Inspirational Short Stories and Encouragement on Life, Love, Friendships and Tough Issues

I am honored that my success has led to being part of the inspiration for this book and the success of the author. I hope all our successes continue to inspire the young people who look up to us.

— Soulja Boy, recording artist

Christopher Combates provides tools that teens can use to design the life they want. It's exciting to find that we possess the power within ourselves to draw in great relationships with parents, friends and teachers, an interesting life, happiness, and opportunities galore.

— Kristine Kouyoumjian,
high school junior, professional tennis player

I am most impressed with Christopher Combates and this excellent book. Teens everywhere are sure to find this book a real asset not only for "having and getting," but for "being and becoming." Way to go, Christopher!

— Tony Perri,
film producer, *Serotonin Rising*

This wonderful book by Chris Combates supports the belief that if everyone used the Law of Attraction correctly, the planet would be a better place for us all! Ever since Christopher told me about the Law of Attraction, it has changed my life for the better. It can change your life, too.

— Jamal Cummings, age 16

I am proud to be associated with such a courageous young man, who is bringing the Law of Attraction to teenagers. This commonly overlooked and underutilized law will change the lives of millions of young people worldwide because of Chris's commitment to awaken them to its power.

— Louis Lautman,
Executive Producer of *The YES Movie*,
founder of Young Entrepreneur Society

The Law of Attraction for Teens feels like it was written just for me. It showed me how to attract more good things into my life, like friends and good grades, and how to deal with the stuff that wasn't helping me to achieve my goals. Now, I'm not afraid to set my standards high because I know I can reach them!

— Mary Burt, age 16

Christopher Combates' book is full of wisdom, so if you are ready to attract wealth from the inside out, read this book!

— Farrah Gray,
syndicated columnist and bestselling author of
Reallionaire and *Get Real, Get Rich*

So many teens feel powerless, but that is a myth. True power lies within, and this book will help teens access their power and use it to shape their lives for the good of all.

— Margit Crane, M.Ed.,
author, *How to Train Your Parents in 5 Days or Less:
A Handbook for Teens*

At times, my life felt like it was spinning out of control with schoolwork, sports, my social life and other demands. But after reading *The Law of Attraction for Teens*, I finally feel like I'm in the driver's seat. Every teen should read this book.

— Evan Stone, age 15

In this excellent book, the author skillfully helps teens use the Law of Attraction to clarify and attract more of what they want, and to eliminate those things that are counterproductive to positive living. When discipline and goal-setting are added to this mix, superior results are bound to follow.

— Chris Cucchiara,
founder, Chris Cucchiara's Youth-Fit Camp, and author,
*Lessons from the Gym for Teens: 5 Secrets to Gaining Control
of Your Life*

Even as the invincible teenager who accomplished so much and had the perfect college application resume, little did I know that my life could turn upside-down, leaving me overwhelmed with feelings of rejection and the need to fulfill expectations. *The Law of Attraction for Teens* helped me remember what I am capable of, gain control, and get back in action.

— Emily M. Yeo,
winner, National Guild Piano Auditions,
and golfer, SCPGA Junior Tour, age 22

At Kids Korps USA, we know the value of helping teens show up in life and feel needed, wanted, and valued. Learning how to shape their desires and then bring them to fruition is most important. This book can help them see their role in changing themselves, their communities, and the world!

— Joani Wafer,
founder, Kids Korps, USA

The Law of Attraction for Teens is a must-have guidebook for creating the life you want. The author provides tools to empower you to take charge of your destiny, resulting in better relationships, grades, and attitudes, and more joy in life!

— Susan M. Heim,
co-author, *Chicken Soup for the Soul: All in the Family*

Christopher Combates' knowledge of the Law of Attraction combined with his life experience as a teenager provides an opportunity for young adults to relate and apply life-changing tools for creating their optimum lives. *The Law of Attraction for Teens* is one of the greatest gifts a teenager can receive.

— Nikki Cortez,
Law of Attraction coach

In this excellent book, teenager Christopher Combates provides expert advice for teens on using the Law of Attraction, and the knowhow to empower teens to take control of their destiny. This should be required reading for all teens!

— Marla Martenson,
author, *Excuse Me, Your Soul Mate Is Waiting*

This excellent book is sure to help teens design the future they desire. Attract, design, apply!

—Aura Imbarus,
author, *101 Great Ways to Make the World a Totally Awesome Place*

This book gives teens the tools to attract what they want and get rid of what they don't want! When they follow the steps in this book, they can improve themselves and their lives.

— Scott Ricke, M.D.,
author, *The Thinking Teen's Guide to Weight Management*

It's good to know that I can have a hand in making my life better and that I can send some of the crappy things in my life on their way!

— Connor Botts, 15

The LAW *of* ATTRACTION
for TEENS

*How to Attract More
of the Good Stuff
and Get Rid of
the Bad Stuff*

CHRISTOPHER A. COMBATES

TEEN TOWN PRESS

Cover design by Sandy Reber, Reber Creative
Illustrations by Andrew Richard Ward

www.TeenTownPress.com

If you are unable to order this book from your local bookseller, or wish to order books for your classroom or group, you may order directly from the publisher. Contact us at www.TeenTownPress.com

Teen Town Press is an Imprint of Bettie Youngs Books
www.BettieYoungsBooks.com

Library of Congress Control Number: 2010923392

ISBN: 978-1-936332-29-8

BISAC: Teens/Self-Help

Printed on acid-free paper

Printed in the USA

Contents

Introduction

I am a teenager, just like you. The only difference between you and me is that I came across the Law of Attraction at a very young age and have used it to my advantage. This book was written to give you a similar leg-up. I know you read enough in school, but this information will literally change your life.

Now, after reading that, you might assume I'm a bookworm or spiritual freak, but I'm quite the opposite. I listen to rock and hip hop, have my ear pierced, play video games, and hang out with friends. But the Law of Attraction inspired me so much that I just had to write about it. I feel that it is my mission to tell other teenagers about the ways their lives *can* change for the better.

It doesn't matter if you're a prep, skater, nerd or anything in between. If you learn to use the Law of Attraction consciously, it will improve your life tremendously. There is no need to be a bookworm in order to understand and use this powerful technique. In fact, I only recently began to read for enjoyment. So, hold on my fellow teens, and stick with me through a few more pages!

How the Law of Attraction Came into My Life

I came across the Law of Attraction through a movie known as *The Secret.* (I saw an ad for it on the Internet!) Although *The Secret* is not a common teenage movie, every teen should watch it. Not only is it an awesome way to spend an hour and a half, but it is also a wonderful introduction to the Law of Attraction. Every second of it is jam-packed with useful information that will change your life for the better. It is also very inspirational. If you would like a visual introduction to the Law of Attraction, you might want to watch *The Secret* while reading this book.

After viewing the movie a number of times, I decided I needed to research more about this topic, so I Googled the "Law of Attraction." Many useful links popped up that were filled with book titles and YouTube videos. I started with YouTube, which was a goldmine of information (and still is today). Michael Losier was one of the first names I came across on YouTube, and his insightful and helpful videos pulled me even further into the subject. Before I knew it, I was watching these videos on a consistent basis.

As my knowledge and awareness of the Law of Attraction grew, and my life began to change, I decided to start reading actual books on the topic. I started with *The Secret* by Rhonda Byrne, which is based on the movie. Then I read *Law of Attraction* by Michael Losier because I liked his YouTube videos so much. This was the first time I could literally see my life improving due to reading a book. Many books followed these two, including those by Esther and Jerry Hicks. (See "Suggested Resources" at the end of this book.) Reading these wonderful bestsellers changed my view on life in every way.

Shortly thereafter, the idea popped into my head to write this book. I had never seen any of this information directed toward teens, and it was a turning point for me. I'm hoping to change other teenage lives in the same way these books and videos changed mine.

How the Law of Attraction Affects Your Life

Whether you know it, understand it, or believe it, the Law of Attraction is affecting you every second of every day of every year. It affects all aspects of your life, from the relationships you have with friends, down to the grade on your test in math class. This law is just as real and as important as the law of gravity.

In the following chapters, I will define the Law of Attraction and provide an introduction to the subject. You will learn how important your thoughts and feelings are. You'll also learn the first steps you can take to get rid of the *bad* stuff, while attracting more of the *good* stuff into your life. Everything from school and friends to your family and future will be changed for the better. And it will occur easily and joyfully, after you apply the information in this book.

Chapter 1

The Basics of the Law of Attraction

Creation is always happening. Every time an individual has a thought, or a prolonged, chronic way of thinking, they're in the creation process. Something is going to manifest out of those thoughts.

Michael Beckwith

The Law of Attraction, Power of Intention, Thought Manifestation, Creation Process, Art of Allowing, and Power of Belief all mean one thing: **What you think about, you bring about.** In other words, what you think about the most eventually becomes a part of your life. I'm sure this sounds a little weird, but it affects you in more ways than you're aware of. Every single thought that passes through your head affects your reality and the situations you experience in life. This is possible because...

Thoughts Create Feelings

Feelings and emotions are what the Law of Attraction is truly about. Feelings and emotions attract results to you. Every thought creates a specific feeling, which is either positive or negative. This specific feeling attracts situations, people, and objects that match it. One of the main ways to describe the Law of Attraction is to say "like attracts like." So, if you are thinking negative thoughts, you are feeling negative emotions. When you are feeling negative emotions, you are attracting negative things! And it works the same way with positive thoughts.

Thoughts → Feelings/Emotions → Results
So...

Negative Thoughts → Negative Feelings/Emotions → Negative Results

Positive Thoughts → Positive Feelings/Emotions → Positive Results

It is quite simple once you understand it!

How Do I Know This "Law" Is Real?

Honestly, when I first learned about the Law of Attraction, I thought it was complete nonsense. I had never heard of it before, and all of a sudden this movie was telling me that my thoughts attracted situations, objects, and people! It seemed like some sort of crazy scam, or maybe just a bunch of old people who *really* believed in magic. But, despite my doubts, I was still curious about the whole concept, and I couldn't seem to stop myself from investigating further. It's like when someone walks by with purple hair, and you think it looks ridiculous, but you still can't stop yourself from checking it out! That's how I felt with the Law of Attraction at first. But when the results I desired began to show up in my life, my whole opinion changed!

As I became more interested in the subject, Internet research took up most of my time. I was shocked to find that many famous and extremely brilliant people in history were aware of the Law of Attraction! Here are a few people you may have heard of, who clearly state their wisdom and understanding regarding the Law of Attraction.

Whether you think you can or can't, either way you are right.

— Henry Ford

Imagination is everything. It is the preview of life's coming attractions.

— Albert Einstein

All that we are is the result of what we have thought.
— Siddhartha Gautama ("Buddha")

I am no longer cursed by poverty because I took possession of my own mind, and that mind has yielded me every material thing I want, and much more than I need. But this power of mind is a universal one, available to the humblest person as it is to the greatest.
— Andrew Carnegie

You create your own universe as you go along.
— Winston Churchill

The greatest discovery of my generation is that human beings can alter their lives by altering their attitudes of mind.
— William James

These are only a few of the people in history who knew and practiced the Law of Attraction. Two modern celebrities who openly believe in this law are Oprah and Will Smith.

But the best way to "prove" the Law of Attraction is to experience it for yourself. I knew the law was real when I could no longer deny the impact it was having in my life.

If hearing about what others think of the Law of Attraction is not convincing enough, read the next section about bad days. I'm positive you will begin to say, "Ahhh, this is starting to make sense." What do you have to lose but a few minutes of your spare time? If you take the time to read this book, front to back, you will be smiling more than ever before. There is a reason I made this book short and simple!

Bad Days

Have you ever had a bad day? Everyone has! You open up your eyes to a blasting alarm clock and realize you set it one hour behind. Now you're completely late for school. While getting up, you remember that you didn't do your homework last night because of after-school activities. As you run to the bathroom to hop in the shower, you stub your toe on the side of the door. It's been five minutes since waking up, and the bed is already calling you back. With this *thought* in mind, you turn on the shower and wait for it to get warm. But it doesn't get warm. Someone used all the hot water! I could go on and on about bad days, but I think you get the picture.

The reason we have bad days are due to either an unawareness of the Law of Attraction or a failure to apply it. Why? One bad incident can change your mindset for the day and create a snowball effect of negative thoughts. Negative thoughts create negative feelings, and negative feelings attract negative situations. It can be a never-ending process—until you change your thoughts.

Just because you woke up late does not mean the rest of your day has to be horrible. You can change your thoughts in a split second and have the best day of your life. Many people say it's hard to think good thoughts when your toe is sore, you're freezing in the shower, and you're late for school. I am here to tell you that it can be done, and it is worth it. Of course, if you like having bad days, go ahead and keep thinking those negative thoughts—that is entirely up to you!

But if, like me, you'd rather enjoy a good day, you'll want to start to employ the positive methods and techniques in this book that can change your way of thinking completely. When you change your way of thinking, you change the way you feel, and when you change the way you feel, your life changes!

The more you remember this throughout the day, the more control you will gain in your life. Bad days will become an extremely rare occasion and, sooner or later, almost an impossibility.

It's Just a Coincidence ... or Is It?

When was the last time you experienced a coincidence? Perhaps you ran into a friend you were just talking about, or you had a song stuck in your head and then heard it on the radio. It happens all the time. People think coincidences occur by chance. But they are simply the Law of Attraction displayed in a small aspect of your life.

Following is a list of commonly used words and phrases that are, in fact, evidence of the Law of Attraction. While many people consider these occurrences completely random, they'd be shocked if they only knew the power of their minds.

- Coincidence
- Luck
- Out-of-the-blue
- Destiny
- Meant to be
- Karma
- That's the way the cookie crumbles
- Speak of the devil

A while ago, I had a question that I wanted to ask my friend, Erik. It was on my mind for a while, but I never got around to asking it. When I "coincidentally" ran into him, we chatted for a bit about school, cracked some jokes, and laughed. As I was about to ask him my question, he immediately switched to the issue I was going to talk about! I replied, "Wow, I was just going to ask you about that. What a coincidence!" This is a common example of this wonderful law at work.

After this incident, I began to explain the Law of Attraction to my friend. He became very interested, and now uses it every day in his teenage life.

It's All About Vibes

You experience a coincidence when enough attention, energy, and focus is put into a certain thought or group of thoughts. By doing this, your mood or feeling shifts to match what you're thinking about. A feeling emits a "vibration" or "vibe." When this "vibe" is sent out, the Law of Attraction performs its one and only job: to match vibrations with situations, people, and objects that are in harmony with it. In other words, *the vibration you send out attracts the results you receive in your life.* Humans and their minds are way more powerful than you think. Once you learn to control your vibration, life will change in ways you can't even imagine.

Every thought, feeling, and action has a vibration or frequency. Everything in this world is vibration. All particles of matter are vibrating at a certain frequency. Now, remember, like attracts like. So if your positive thoughts are vibrating at a high frequency, your actions are also vibrating at a high frequency.

Your *emotions* are key to finding out what frequency you're vibrating on and, therefore, what you're attracting into your life. Positive emotions attract more of the "good stuff," while negative emotions attract the "bad stuff." So, clearly, identifying and managing your emotions is going to be key in attracting the things you want instead of the things you don't want.

As soon as you feel a negative emotion, do anything you can to make yourself feel better. Put on your favorite music, or think about something you love or are grateful for. This will help dramatically.

At this point you may be asking, "Well, that sounds great, but I'm not always sure which emotions are positive and which ones are negative. How can I tell?"

Positive and Negative Vibes

Simply put, positive emotions make you feel good; negative emotions make you feel bad. And remember, an emotion/feeling, whether negative or positive, determines your vibration, and thus the things and results that you are going to attract into your life. To make it more clear, here are two diagrams that contain a variety of positive and negative vibes.

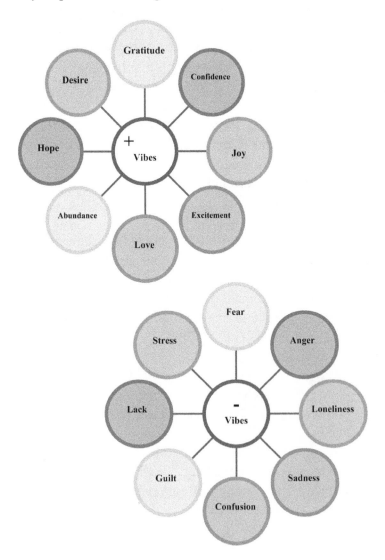

Identify each of the emotions on these charts, and recognize how they make you feel: good or bad, positive or negative. Obviously, the emotions in the diagram on the top left make you feel excellent, and those on the right make you feel horrible. This raises a common question: What if negative emotion didn't exist? There would be no negative vibes! Wouldn't that be wonderful?

Surprisingly, the answer is *no*! Without negative emotion, positive emotion wouldn't exist. It is a fact of life: Without the bad, there is no good. Think about it—comparison is always needed.

The brilliant option of *choice* allows you to choose which emotions you experience, at least, most of the time. Of course, you will feel the negatives on occasion. We're all human, and no one is perfect. And, as I have said, the negatives are totally necessary, because they provide the contrast that helps you figure out what you *do* want.

The idea is to feel negative emotions as briefly as possible.

The longer you hold a negative emotion or feeling, the more negativity you will attract. Humans have emotions and feelings to let us know if we are experiencing something harmful or helpful. They tell us whether the vibe we are sending matches what we truly want and desire.

Begin to view negative emotions as warning signals. Once you realize this, you will understand that there is no point to feeling these emotions for long periods of time. The minute you feel a negative vibe/feeling/emotion, stop and ask yourself, "So what *do* I want?" This technique was taught to me by Law of Attraction expert, Michael J. Losier. When you switch your focus from what you don't want to what you do want, your vibration changes. And when your vibration changes, your results change.

So, How Do You Change Your Vibration?

Again, begin focusing on what you *do* want, rather than what you *don't* want. Whenever you're experiencing a negative emotion, you are focusing on what you don't want.

- I don't want to fail my test.
- I don't want to lose the race.
- I don't want to make a mistake.

By thinking this way, you are moving farther and farther away from what you *do* want!

Many people say, "Complaining and moping won't get you anywhere." The truth is that it *will* get you somewhere: into a *worse* situation!

The more attention, energy, and focus you put into what you don't want, the more you receive that which you don't want! And, conversely, when you put your attention, energy, and focus on what you DO want, those things will increasingly start to show up in your life.

Try turning your negative thoughts into positive ones by focusing on what you *do* want. For example, the negative statements above could be turned into the following:

- I want to do well on my test.
- I want to improve my running time.
- I want to make a good choice.

Can you see the difference? Which way of thinking is going to make you feel better?

You're Already Manifesting

Manifest, manifesting, and *manifestation* are words that will be used a lot in this book. If you do not already know the meaning of these words, read the following:

Manifest: Becoming aware to our senses or to bring into reality; create.

In teen terms…

Manifest: To get what you want.

When talking about the Law of Attraction, the term "manifestation" is used to describe the process of achieving, creating, and attracting one's desires. Manifesting is the goal of every Law of Attraction-related action. Throughout this book, you will learn the art of manifesting, as well as methods and activities that make the process easy. By the end of this book, you will have the tools and awareness to manifest anything you want!

My friend Mark used the Law of Attraction to attract his ideal car. Take a look at how he did it!

How Mark Manifested His Ideal Car

Mark: Age 16, 11th Grade

My friend, Mark, has always been into cars. He would study them and talk about them constantly. Cars were always on his mind, even before he was old enough to drive. When the time finally came for Mark to get his license, he took the test confidently and passed with ease.

Mark's next task was to buy a car. He had been working a side job for a year or two, just for this purpose. While working, he began to visualize (without even realizing it) the car that he wanted: a Mazda 3. After saving his paychecks for a while and combining his earnings with birthday money, Mark had five thousand dollars. His parents said that whatever he made, they would match. So, in reality, he had ten thousand. Mark was excited; he could feel the positive emotions running through him. He continued to visualize his ideal Mazda 3. After a week or two of searching, he found a used Mazda 3 for sale, a half-hour away. The price was set for nine thousand five hundred dollars! Mark said it happened totally "out of the blue." When I heard this, I laughed.

Mark's parents agreed to take a ride with him to look at this car. When they arrived, Mark discovered that the car's interior was blue; this was not what he wanted. His ideal color was black, but he decided to settle.

As they were about to negotiate the deal, the man who was selling it shouted, "Fifteen thousand!" They did not have fifteen thousand! They tried to negotiate, but it didn't work. Mark ended up riding home in his parents' car, rather than his new Mazda. He was extremely disappointed.

When Mark got home, he stayed positive even though it seemed his dream was broken. A few days later, he decided to search for a Mazda one last time. He looked online at a used car dealership. There was a Mazda 3 selling for 9,000 dollars only five minutes away! He immediately ran to his parents and told them the news. They had some doubts, but agreed to look at it. Mark's ideal Mazda kept driving through his mind. On the way to look at the car, he was extremely excited and filled with energy.

When they arrived at the dealership, Mark hopped out and walked over to the car. The outside looked great, but he was nervous about looking inside. When he built up enough courage, he decided to open the door. The car had a black interior just like Mark wanted! Everything about the car was ideal, so Mark and his parents bought the car on the spot. Mark continues to drive that Mazda today. Whenever I see it, I think: Law of Attraction in action!

Mark's story shows how the Law of Attraction works in mysterious ways. Staying positive through hard situations will lead to your desire.

Conclusion

Remaining unaware of the Law of Attraction is the same as walking somewhere without any shoes. You can still get to where you want to go, but it will be awfully hard, and will take a lot longer.

This analogy really defines the point of this book. Do you normally see people walking down the street without any shoes? Probably not, and one of the reasons they wear shoes is because they learned at a young age that it's easier to use them than not to. Most people discovered before age six that it is easier to get somewhere if you're wearing shoes (especially when you are walking through rough patches)! And that is why I am trying to get this message across to young adults—so that they can start to live their lives the easier way, sooner rather than later!

It's possible that you still may be skeptical about the Law of Attraction, and that's okay and natural. But I'm asking you to be open-minded and just try out this idea. See if you can notice the Law of Attraction working in your everyday life.

Almost all of the Law of Attraction books, videos, and movies I've seen are aimed at adults. It is time for a change. Kids and teenagers need to learn about this as well, so that by the time we are fully grown, we are experts at using this magnificent information to create magnificent lives. When we can do that, the quote "Anything is possible" will be more accurate than ever.

Wouldn't it be great if we could introduce this law to everyone as early as possible? If all of humanity knew about the Law of Attraction, imagine how peaceful this world would be. If people realized that when they think negative or harmful thoughts, they are only hurting themselves, the world would become a much more positive place for all of us.

Chapter 2

The Three-Step
Manifestation Process

*Your thoughts and your feelings create your life. It
will always be that way. Guaranteed.*

Lisa Nichols

Before we go any further, I want to introduce the most useful tool in this book. This will allow you to begin manifesting your desires as soon as possible.

I have created a set of exercises inspired by Michael Losier, which are basically a teen version of those in his bestselling book, *Law of Attraction,* and are beneficial beyond belief. I will explain how to apply these exercises to the rest of this book and how they will impact your life if you follow through with them. These exercises are simple and short, but will improve your life more than any ordinary school assignment. They will shift your mindset into the positive aspects of life. You will begin attracting your actual desires instead of the things you don't want. **I'm trying to tell you that it is worth it to try this out!** Obviously, no one wants to do more "work" than they have to, but when the results are shown, you will realize that these exercises are *far* from "work."

During a chat with Michael, I explained to him the issues I was having with my dad. The methods we used to shift my vibrations worked in ways you cannot imagine. I will show you the exact exercises I did with the actual problems I had with my dad so you can see how it truly affected my personal relationship.

Step 1: Finding Your Desire

On a sheet of paper, make two columns. On the left side, list the things you *don't* want. On the right side, list the things you *do* want. The purpose of the negative side is to help you realize what you truly want. Without the negative, there is no positive. Many teens (and a great many adults, for that matter) know exactly what they don't want, but have no idea what they do want. It is essential that you write what you don't want because it will be easier to find what you do want. Your true desires are exact opposites of the things you want to avoid.

After you have written down the things you don't want on the negative side, you can cross out/fold over the left side. From that point on, focus only on what you DO want. Once you have this list of your true wants, you should review it every day at least once. Keep it in your head throughout the day and make note of how it begins to change your life. It is a great idea to review this list before bed. Your brain will focus on the positives while you sleep. Here is what my list looked like when I wanted to have a better relationship with my dad:

My Ultimate: <u>Relationship with My Dad</u>

Negative **Things I don't want**	Positive **Things I do want**
~~He expects too much.~~	Happy with what I do, as it is.
~~He doesn't "know" me.~~	Understands me and my interests.
~~Main problem of the family.~~	Brings harmony to my family.
~~He is never serious, always joking.~~	He is serious when the time is right.
~~Does not see my potential.~~ ~~He sees me as a "kid."~~	Can see how much true potential I have.
~~He doesn't think I work enough.~~	Sees me as a young adult. Appreciates the amount of work I do.
~~Always nagging me.~~	Has patience and gives me space.

If you don't have a clue about what desire to start with in doing the above exercise, the list of topics below might spur some ideas:

- Relationships (parents, friends, dates)
- Money (part-time job, contests)
- School (grades, teachers, sports)
- Object (car, video game, cell phone)
- Emotions (happy more often, grateful)
- Clothing (any type)
- Social status (wanting more friends, acceptance)
- Life in general (plan out your ideal life)

Step 2: Increasing Your Vibration

Now that you've determined what you want, step two focuses on increasing your positive vibrations. This will help you manifest faster and easier.

Using the items you listed in the "Things I do want" column in Step 1, write a series of sentences using positive and encouraging words that trigger emotions of joy, optimism, and excitement. Example of phrases could be:

- I love knowing that my ultimate_____.
- I'm thrilled at the thought of_____.
- I love noticing myself_____.
- I've determined that_____.
- Create your own, whatever increases your vibes!

Below are the phrases I created about my dad, back when our relationship was a little shaky. Keep in mind that you don't have to have a horrible relationship with someone to use these exercises. The relationship I had with my dad wasn't *that* bad. It was simply the one that needed most work. Writing these few short pages was definitely worth it.

I love knowing that my ultimate relationship with my dad is comfortable and relaxed.

I've determined that my dad will begin to see me as a young adult.

I love the feeling of my dad understanding me and my interests.

I'm thrilled at the thought of my dad having patience and bringing harmony to my family.

I love how it feels when my dad is serious when needed and jokes around when the time is right.

More and more, I begin to see my dad giving me space and leaving me alone when I'm trying to get something done.

Step 3: Allowing

This last step is used to minimize or remove any doubt that what you truly desire will manifest in your life. But in order to successfully manifest that which you desire, you must practice the Art of Allowing. Allowing is the process of believing or "trusting" the Law of Attraction. Without the feeling of belief or trust, you will not *allow* what you desire into your life. It is the last rung on the L.O.A. ladder, right before you hit the top. Once your doubt is gone, your desires will flow to you easily. Most likely, your mind has been programmed by society to think in a certain way:

- "Money is hard to get."
- "School sucks…"
- "It's almost impossible to be successful in your own business."
- "Life's a b**ch."

So, how can you get rid of your doubts? Answer the following questions:

1. Who else has what you want?
2. How many people have it?
3. Write this statement in a way that is believable.

Most likely, there are tons of people who have the situation, relationship, or object that you want, which is proof that you can have it, too. Here's what I wrote in dealing with the situation with my dad:

> Millions of people have great relationships with their dads.
>
> Every day, relationships are being fixed through the Law of Attraction.
>
> I have a good relationship with my mom. I'm sure I can have the same with my dad.
>
> Many of my friends tell me how well they get along with their dads.
>
> I want a better relationship with my dad so that's what I am going to have.

How Chris Manifested the Perfect Mentor

Chris (Myself): Age 16, 11th Grade

I have many personal success stories using the Law of Attraction. My favorite is the attraction of my mentor and friend, Michael Losier. Along with experts such as Lynn Grabhorn and Marla Martenson, Michael was one of the pioneers in making the Law of Attraction known to the general public. Nowadays, there are a number of books on the subject, but at one point not that long ago, his book was one of the few that contained "Law of Attraction" in the title. He is admired by many people all over the world, and his book has been translated into twenty-six languages! Who would have thought that a teenager from New Jersey could end up with this successful man as a mentor?

So, there I was, a fifteen-year-old, studying the Law of Attraction. I had been learning about it for almost two years, but I still had doubts and was not nearly as successful at using the law as I am now. In the course of my studies, I began to watch videos by many of the Law of Attraction gurus, including Esther and Jerry Hicks. Losier's videos, however, were my favorite. They were very informative, and I loved the way he taught.

I eventually ran out of "Michael material" (as I call it) on the Internet, but I felt the need to learn more from him. So—as it always does—the Law of Attraction gave me what matched my vibrations. About a week later, my mom brought home a book that she had purchased for herself: *Law of Attraction*, by Michael J. Losier. At the time, she was in the middle of another self-help book, so I got to read it first! I finished it in about two days, and I was completely inspired. A day later, I decided to start my project creating a Law of Attraction book for teenagers.

My mom then informed me that Michael Losier had a Facebook account. My imagination was kick-started! I began to think, "I should add him as a friend. Maybe I should tell him about my idea. But is that profile really him, and what if he doesn't care about my project?" Despite my doubts, I built up the courage to add him, while daydreaming about the possibilities at the same time. I waited a few days and looked through his profile further. It seemed real, so I decided to message him about my project. I kept my vibrations high, and within a day or two he responded! Michael let me know that he was interested in the project and wanted to know more.

And the rest is history! Michael and I have become friends, and he's been extremely instrumental in helping me use the Law of Attraction.

Still Having Doubts?

Doubt is an emotion that overrides all others. You can feel however you want—happy, joyful, excited, or confident—but at the end of the day, if you refuse to believe, your doubt cancels out most of your positive emotions. I've seen this happen with many of my peers.

When I first began to study the Law of Attraction, it was hard for me to believe, just as it is for many other people. I did some of the exercises, but didn't see a lot of results at first. Then I realized that the reason I wasn't successful was due to the doubt I had in the law itself. The whole idea sounded great, but I still doubted that this law existed. So I said, "Why not just believe it? Even if I'm wrong, what is there to lose?" So I suspended my disbelief long enough to give it a try and began seeing positive results. **And the more belief and trust I gained, the more results I attained.**

Belief is the most important quality required for this to work. Trust this law, and you will begin to see it working all around you.

Now that you've decided that you have nothing to lose and everything to gain, you can begin the process of changing any aspect of your life. The next three chapters specifically address three areas in which you may want to manifest your desire: school, parents, and friends.

Chapter 3

The Law of Attraction
and School

*Change your vibrations,
and you'll change the results you're getting.*

Michael Losier

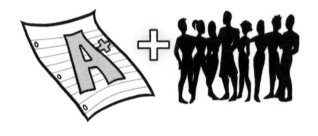

If you are one of the few kids who truly loves and enjoys school to the fullest, good for you. For the rest us, I have some methods to help make the best of your school experience while keeping your grades up at the same time.

My first piece of advice is to start thinking positively about your school year before it even starts. Try to plan out what will take place and how good of a year you will have. Visualize your report cards with high grades on them. A good idea is to take one of your previous report cards, cross out the old grades, and write in your "new" grades. Place this on your wall during the summer, and while you are having fun and enjoying yourself, look forward to how good you will do the next school year.

And while grades are obviously very important in your school career, social interaction is just as significant. During the school year, make sure you have a balance between social and academic aspects. When you find stability between the two, you will succeed.

Besides preparing a "new" report card out of your old one, there are numerous methods for getting your grades back on track if they begin to slip. First, realize that positive thinking through the Law of Attraction will not take the test or do your homework for you; this job relies on the law of ACTION. What the Law of Attraction will do, however, is attract the necessary situations, people, and ideas in order for you to meet your honor roll goal. Begin to align your new and improved positive thoughts with new actions. Keep a positive stream of self-talk running through your head at all times. "This homework is easy." "I'm sure I'll be able to pass this test." "Today is an easy, successful, straight-A school day." These statements may not feel true to you at first, but if you begin to silently repeat them, they will soon be as "real" as anything.

While aligning your actions with your thoughts and keeping positive self-talk running through your mind, remember to always have confidence. You've heard this before, but it's more important than you think: When you literally *believe* you can accomplish your goals, you eventually will!

Everyone knows the nervous feeling you get when you have a test the next day or it is your turn to present to the class. You have those thoughts in the back of your head of failing the test or looking "dumb" in front of your classmates. Although this is a natural reaction, turn these feeling into benefits. Fear actually helps you focus more on what you are doing, if it is thought about in the right way. When your adrenaline starts pumping and your heart begins to race, use it as an extra push of confidence. Realize that it is only making you hone your skills more sharply. Turn those "failing" thoughts into "straight-A thoughts." It's very difficult to score an A when failing thoughts are running through your mind.

The social portion of school can be just as difficult as academics. Drama, fights, who's going out with whom, and what happened at the party last night can really be a problem if you don't know how to handle it. . If drama is becoming a problem, focus on the positives and remove yourself from the situation. By doing this, drama will fade from your life.

Drama is negative, and you attract it into your life through negative emotions. If you remain in a good mood, drama will not find you; keep your mind on excellent thoughts, and you will have great experiences.
Another exercise you can carry out to increase your success and enjoyment in school is to take a piece of paper and write down anything and everything you admire about it. "What I admire about *school*?" you may say. "That is going to be a very short list!" While you may not be used to thinking about the positive aspects of school, I'm sure you have a *few* things...

I am happy that I can see my friends almost every day of the week.

If it wasn't for school, I wouldn't have half the friends I do now.

Many people in this world don't have the opportunity to go to school. I'm thankful that I do.

The more I learn, the brighter my future will be.

True gratitude is an extremely positive emotion. This is just one way to enhance your feelings of thankfulness. Whenever you start to feel frustrated or annoyed because of school, look over this list and really sense the gratitude flowing through you. I'm sure you will feel a lot better, and raise your vibrations at the same time.

This type of list can be made for any situation—school, family, or your part-time job—any branch of your life that needs some positive change.

Now we all know that teachers can get on our nerves, some a little more than others. But it is possible to form a positive relationship with your teachers.

If you get into a class with a teacher you don't "click" with right away, stick it out. It will be a great learning experience. You need to understand that you will not "click" with everyone in this world; people have their differences. Transferring out of a class because you don't like a teacher will simply create more negative vibes than you already have.

You can perform the same gratitude exercise I showed you for school for teachers, too. Focus on their positives, not on their negatives. Focusing on their negatives will only make you more aware of the things that tick you off, which will obviously lead to further problems.

I know teens love to rant about how bad their teachers are, but it's really not worth it. If you hear your friends doing this, realize they are spewing their negative vibes at you. Explain to them why the teacher isn't *that* bad, and give them an example of something you like about him or her. Maybe the teacher gave you extra points or even some good advice on a topic you weren't sure about. Talking trash about the teacher will only make your school experience worse. Trust me, I've made the mistake myself. You'll simply be attracting more negative stuff, both from that particular teacher and in other areas of your life.

In my freshman year of high school, I had an English teacher who could be pretty funny, but he was really short and not a great instructor. As we were taking the midterm exam, my friend decided to write an insult about the teacher on a piece of paper. As he handed it to me, I could *feel* that this was leading to a bad situation. I knew about the Law of Attraction at the time, but I did not take it into real consideration. I was stressed from the midterm and wanted to let loose.

As I read the note, I'll admit that it made me laugh a little. It said: "The leprechaun seems a little moody today, huh?" I wrote back, "Yeah, I think he lost his pot of gold. lol." Now, as I said before, I had a bad feeling or bad vibe about this. Your situations always match your vibrations, and when you're talking negative about someone, your vibes are negative, even though you're laughing and having a good time. You are sending out the message that *negative situations* make you happy, so bring me more!

Before I knew it, another student had taken the note from my friend's desk and handed it to the teacher. At this point, I knew I was screwed. I could see my English teacher turning sour as he read the note. To be honest, I felt bad for him. As you can see, it was a mess of negativity. This wasn't going to turn out good for anyone. To make a long story short, my friends and I were assigned two after-school detentions.

Moral of the story: It won't do anything but attract negative situations and make school that much tougher. If you are having negative feelings about one of your teachers (or anything else at school), quickly find something positive to focus on and raise your vibration!

I use the word "disruptor" because bullies, punks, and drama queens don't do anything but disrupt your vibration. If you are having trouble with disruptors, you have to recognize that you are attracting it. That may be hard to admit, but it's not about blaming yourself. Really, it is not even your fault because you were not aware of the Law of Attraction before. But now that I am explaining it to you, it would be in your best interests and much to your advantage to use it!

Bullies, punks, and drama queens are almost always in a negative vibration. That is why they "disrupt" your positive vibration. Whenever you see or hear them, your vibration begins to drop. This is a natural reaction. Some common thoughts are "What is he going to do now...?" or "Not again!" When you think this way, you lower your vibration to match theirs. This makes you a complete target! At that very moment, you are attracted to each other. The disruptor walks by you and can feel the vibration of fear, annoyance, and frustration. He can see it in your expressions and feel it in your presence. Once you learn to keep your vibrations high around disruptors, they will walk by and not even notice you. Think about it, have you ever seen a bully picking on a kid who is smiling and laughing? If you have, it didn't happen for long.

I have three tips that will remove most, or even all of the disruptors from your life. I have tested this process with many peers from my high school as well as others. It has worked in all scenarios and should work for you. (The example I'm describing involves a bully, but the technique applies to any type of disruptor you may encounter.)

Fear is an *extremely* strong negative emotion (vibe). The more fear you have for bullies, the more you will be harassed and disrupted by them. I have seen many cases of teens solving their bullying problems with this first tip alone. If you are walking through the hallways scared and displaying fearful emotions, you will look like an excellent target for any disruptor. Be confident and strong!

If you are confronted by a bully, put on a classic smile. Even if it is not real, it will create a positive vibe and completely throw off the bully. By doing this you will counter him/her and disrupt his/her negative vibes.

 *positive thoughts*The more positive you are during the confrontation, the quicker it will end. This doesn't mean you have to say anything. Simply hold your smile, think about something that makes you happy, and remove yourself from the situation. Fighting back will simply create a negative environment, leaving you hurt and/or suspended.

If the situation gets serious enough that you have to talk to a teacher, do it. Just remember that putting emphasis, time, and conversation into the topic of bullying will attract more of it to you. So make your decisions wisely. Disruptors always have disruptive friends, and what do you think will happen when his "friends" hear that he is getting in trouble because of you? Now you have a whole new set of disruptors out to mess up your vibes.

If you can handle the situation on your own without violence, you are heading in the right direction. Of course, if the problem turns into physical contact, you should find help immediately.

Age 17, 11th Grade

My friend, Brian, had many issues with disruptors in the past. He was criticized and picked on for the clothes he wore, the way he talked, and his body. If there was one kid who had it bad, it was him. My mission as a young teen was to turn his life around. I began by introducing Brian to the Law of Attraction, while at the same time teaching him the three tips I have just mentioned. Within the first week of changing his thoughts, Brian began to "turn invisible" to disruptors. I continued to coach Brian for about a year. Each day he improved. I could even see his style changing. He was happier, and the soccer coach asked him to play for the team! Everything was going great for him.

Today, Brian continues to use the Law of Attraction deliberately in his life. He is quite popular in school, and for all the right reasons. Once he removed his fear, smiled more, and kept positive thoughts (which made his vibration rise), his life became much easier.

Knowledge of the Law of Attraction can be very useful for you and your sports teams. Putting Law of Attraction principles into practice will give the players motivation, and your team will gain the power of the universe on "your side." Most of the time, successful sports teams are already using the Law of Attraction without knowing it! The pep talks before the game are usually full of encouragement and positive motivation.

Get your team involved with this awesome power. Bribe them with a "better" season so they will listen to what you have to say. If you have open-minded coaches, you can let them know about the Law of Attraction.

As a young adult, life after high school is probably never too far from your mind. What will you do, where will you go, and who will you become? Whether you are already determined to go to college or would rather go right to work, it is totally up to you (and, to some extent, your parents). This section is written for teens who want to go on to college.

Thinking about going to college can be daunting, but choosing and applying to your ideal college can be even more so. This process can be made much easier by deliberately using the Law of Attraction. As you have probably seen in the halls of your own school, many teens worryabout this big change. Worry is a strong negative emotion, and should be felt as little as possible. Worry only draws negative attention to the topic that you're worrying about. So remember to stay confident while looking for and applying to colleges and feel reassured that the Law of Attraction will handle the situation.

An awesome way to attract your ideal college is to create the don't want/do want worksheet that I showed you in Chapter 2. By becoming clear about the qualities you *do* want in your college, the chances of finding an awesome school are increased dramatically. I have put my own Ideal College worksheet below. Take a look and use it as an example.

Negative   Positive

~~Not being accepted into any college.~~	Being accepted into almost every college I apply to.
~~Not sure about what types of colleges I'd like to attend.~~	Know exactly what types of colleges I'd like to attend.
~~Receiving no scholarships.~~	Receiving tons of scholarships.
~~Horrible dorm rooms in the colleges I get accepted to.~~	Awesome, ideal dorm rooms throughout the college.
~~Extremely expensive courses~~	Whole college experience is easily affordable.

If you apply the advice in this chapter, school will become much more enjoyable, both academically and socially!

Throughout this book, you will see an underlying theme of "being positive," and that's truly what it's all about! In every situation you encounter in life, try to see the positives. No matter how "terrible" things may seem, there is always at least one positive aspect. So by going to school every day with a positive mindset, life will begin changing rapidly. Think positively, feel positively, and experience a positive life!

Christopher A. Combates

Chapter 4

The Law of Attraction and Parents

*Loving the members of your family naturally teaches
you to love and care for the world you live in.*

Marla Martenson

The family you are born into is one of the few factors that *cannot* be created during your lifetime through this beautiful law, but you can improve your relationship with your family tremendously. Your parents were your first mentors, companions, and role models. Parents can get annoying, and siblings can become frustrating, but at the end of the day they are still your family.

Think about it: You are with your family more than anyone else. Most likely, you have spent *at least* fifty percent of your time with them up to now. So why not clear up all the issues as soon as you can? It will make your life at home so much more enjoyable. After living with people for that amount of time, it is easy to forget their good qualities. The three-step exercises I presented in Chapter 2 will bring their good qualities back into the picture.

The Law of Attraction can improve any relationship, but especially those between you and your relatives. Before I studied the law, I barely got along with my dad, as you read earlier in this book. But through my reading and with the help of Michael J. Losier, I have discovered methods and techniques that have greatly improved our relationship. This book provides the same resources and information that I used. If you absorb all of this advice and apply it, you will be able to create any relationship you desire.

Parents

Parents, oh parents. Where in the world to start? Well, first off, without them, you wouldn't be reading this book. That right there should trigger great appreciation. No matter how annoying, stubborn, or whatever you may think they are, they are the reason you're here.

Parents spend, on average, more than a *quarter-million dollars* on raising their child from birth to adulthood. That's a little fun fact for you to consider the next time you feel like cursing them out. Simply realizing how much they do for you on a daily basis will increase your positive vibrations effortlessly. I have seen all sorts of issues become solved through this simple initial step. In my family alone, the vibration of appreciation has helped many issues and concerns.

Like I said before, my dad and I didn't have a truly horrible relationship, but it was the one that annoyed me the most. So I decided to complete the exercises about him first. It is a smart idea to perform them on all of your family members, like your brothers and sisters.

Freedom = Happiness

A major part of growing up is attaining more free time and making your own decisions. This is possibly your most important goal as you mature. I know it is mine! Breaking away from your parents' full control and living your own life, after all, is the ultimate goal of growing up.

That is why 90 percent of the disagreements between you and your family have probably been about your doing what you want to do—your freedom. I bet there have been numerous times when you have felt held back by your parents. That seems to be common ground for just about every teen. Your parents are focusing on keeping you safe and healthy—and you can't blame them for that because it is their instinct. At the same time, your young mind is thinking of adventurous ways to experience new things. I know how you feel.

Many teens don't understand this about parents: There is no point in arguing with them about their decisions! I know this is the easiest way out, and you think it will get you somewhere, but I'm here to tell you that you're wrong. I used to be the exact same way, but after studying the Law of Attraction and viewing my peers' situations, I began to understand one very important principle: **What you resist persists.** As you push against what you don't want, you add power to it. Arguing with your parents only puts more attention, energy, and focus on a negative thing. So refrain from arguing and start negotiating.

Positively Negotiating with Your Parents

There are numerous methods to "get your way" besides arguing and complaining. The more you argue and complain about your situation, the more you will attract what you're arguing and complaining about! The Law of Attraction is always checking in on you, feeling your vibration, and then matching it. That is its job, of course. You may ask, "Why can't we manifest things instantly?" Think about it: have you ever thought in detail about something really bad, such as death or disease? I'm sure you have. Now what would happen if that manifested instantly? In the long run, it is a good thing that thoughts manifest over time. If you think arguing will get your way ("If I stomp my feet enough, they'll give me what I want!"), here is another way to look at it: Let's say you just hit eighteen, and now you want to take out a loan for college. Do you think you can go to the bank and stomp your feet and yell, "Can I please just have a loan!"? Of course not. So now is a great time to learn how to get your way through positive actions and words. Complaining will never work in the long run—not with your parents, and not in your adult life.

So if complaining is not the way to get what you want, what should you do instead? Negotiate, and always with Law of Attraction principles in mind. I have formed a set of guidelines that can be applied when negotiating with your parents. They have been tested on various peers and in my own life, and they always seem to work.

1. Before asking, visualize your parents' reaction.

Most of the time, we as teenagers think our parents will deny our request if it is out of the ordinary. It makes us nervous to ask for things such as going to a concert with a friend or maybe even a weekend away from home because we picture our parents saying no. The new you will visualize your parents saying yes. They will merely ask for details about when, how, and where.

2. Keep a calm, respectful tone.

The first thing a parent observes is your tone of voice. If you start off the conversation with a mad, loud tone, your parents are already setting up to reject what you want. Obviously, it can be a little frustrating, but stick it out and stay cool. Also, many teens tend to ask their parents for something by whining. Whining is another form of complaining, and all it does is create more negative vibrations, which will eventually attract more of the stuff you're whining about! Whether you choose to use the method I have outlined here or not, refrain from complaining or whining.

3. Begin the conversation with something positively off-topic.

Kick off the conversation with something that'll make them smile, such as a good grade on a test, how well you did at practice after school, or just throw them a compliment. But don't make it too obvious. Kissing up to them will expose that you are up to something. If you learn what makes your parents smile without making it obvious, you're set.

4. Inch toward your actual question.

As you are chatting with your parent(s), begin to move toward the important question you have for them. Only talk about positive subjects. If your parents seem to be in a bad mood, or they keep bringing up negative topics, *stop and ask them another time*. It is very unlikely that they will say yes to your question while in a bad mood (vibe).

5. If everything *feels* right, ask them your important question.

If the situation truly feels right, and you can sense your parents' positive vibes, go for it. There is a high chance you will hear the word "YES"! Now, I'm not saying this guideline process will guarantee a yes from your parents every time, but I *can* guarantee that your chances of receiving a yes will increase dramatically. The Law of Attraction cannot *magically* make your parents agree with the freedoms you want or see you as the most deserving son or daughter in the world. In order for that to happen, you need to *make them happy*. Making your parents happy is something you should learn how to do easily and frequently since they have full control over your freedom until you are eighteen. So it is a smart idea to create a great relationship with them. Also, remember the earlier discussion about gratitude—your parents have done a lot for you, and doing what you can to make them happy shows your appreciation.

By increasing the positive vibes flowing between you and your parents, you will increase the amount of freedom you have. The general status of your relationship will also improve. This will partially determine how happy you are as a teen. What's one thing all teens want? To do what they want to do, when they want to do it! And your parents decide how much of this you deserve.

How Alina Attracted More Freedom

Alina: Age 15, 10th Grade

My good friend Alina always had problems with her parents. She used to rant how they never let her out of the house and treated her like a baby. Before I knew about the Law of Attraction, I would chat with her about the topic and sympathize with her problem. After I became aware, enough was enough. She was one of the first people to whom I taught this law. I told her how I had started to positively negotiate with my parents, as well as the art of positive thinking and feeling, and the results I was getting. She began to practice these techniques and, within a month, major results were revealed.

Instead of pouting and arguing with her parents about what she did *not* like, Alina focused on their positive qualities. Although it was quite difficult at first, she began to appreciate everything they do and have done for her.

To make a (great) long story short, Alina now has more freedom than anyone I know. Last time I talked to her, she was staying over at a friend's house in a town I never heard of—something her parents would never have let her do before!

Your Parents' Main Concern Is Your Safety!

You probably hear this statement all the time, but when you really start to appreciate it, things will change. "Strict parents" are simply concerned for your health, safety, and well-being. So the goal is to create the vibration of health, safety, and well-being! By doing this, you will comfort your parents, while at the same time beginning to attract those qualities to you. It is a win/win situation.

How do you think your parents *feel* when you walk up to them and ask, in an immature, whiny voice, *"Can I go to the beach with my friends tomorrow... please!?"*

Right off the bat they're thinking, N-O. That is the response a lot of my friends received. I thought to myself, "Why are my parents more relaxed than theirs?" I figured out that the way I ask my parents is totally different. I realized my peers were putting out uncomfortable, *alert vibrations* to their parents. Alert vibrations are vibes that trigger your parents to feel that the situation is unhealthy, unsafe, and/or harmful to their child. So the objective is to *stop creating alert vibrations* and begin to *create comfort vibrations*.

The amount of comfort vibrations you put out to your parents will determine how much they trust you and allow you to do what you want. What vibes are your parents picking up?

Alert Vibrations

Alert vibrations are negative vibes that many teens emit to their parents on a daily basis. They are one of the main reasons for teen letdowns. Within a second or two of sensing an alert vibration, one word pops into your parents' head: NO. The word "no" is very negative to most teens; "no" is what keeps you from doing what you want to do. Almost all teens are unaware that alert vibrations can be the main cause of hearing "no." When you stop sending these vibes, your chance of a receiving a "yes" skyrockets.

Alert vibrations are caused by the misunderstanding of the right way to talk to parents. It is quite simple. When you beg your parents instead of asking, or when you act immature, your parents get a strong "red flag" feeling. Their natural "parenting instincts" kick in. They begin to keep you from doing whatever you want to do (freedom). Below, I have listed some actions that tend to send strong alert vibrations. Read through them and take note on which ones occur in your everyday life. Be honest.

- Having an attitude
- Nervousness
- Begging "Please, please!"
- Asking ALL the time
- Lying about what you want to do

Comfort Vibrations

Comfort vibrations are *positive* vibes that few teens emit to their parents. Comfort vibrations can also be called "yes" vibrations. When you send more of them, you will receive more "yes" responses! When you begin to emit more of these, rather than alert vibes (aka "no" vibrations), your results will change. You and your parents will have a much better relationship and, at the same time, you will gain more freedom. Parents love to sense comfort vibes releasing from their child. Comfort vibes make parents happy because they feel their child is safe and secure.

Basically, the happier you keep your parents, the more freedom and happiness you will have. I know it can be frustrating at times, but let's face it, that's life. If you focus on the positive and send out comfort vibes as much as you can, the Law of Attraction will match you. In time, you will begin to understand how much this truth affects your teenage life.

Just as there are certain actions that create alert vibrations, there are also actions that tend to create comfort vibrations. Here is a short list of thoughts and actions that send strong comfort vibes.

- Confidently believing your parents will say yes
- Keeping a calm, respectful tone
- Maturely negotiating
- Keeping your mind and conversation positive
- Showing how much you appreciate your parents

Conclusion

Be aware that every parent is different. Everyone's ideal parent-teen relationship will take varied amounts of time to achieve. If this does not happen right away, stay positive. It is only a matter of time before your ideal relationship will happen. Some parents take longer than others. I've heard stories of people changing their relationships with a snap of a finger, and others taking months upon months. Everyone's outcome will not be the same.

Personally, after performing the exercises with my dad, it took around a week for me to see some results. Whenever this happens for you, recognize it, and be thankful for the outcome. The more gratitude you feel and show, the better. This will, in turn, bring more of that feeling to you. Whatever situation you feel gratitude for, realize that the Law of Attraction is matching that feeling "vibration" and arranging new events, circumstances, and objects that will bring more of that feeling to you. So, it is not just that it is kind to be thankful, but it will improve your life and attract more of what you want! Whenever you have the chance to be thankful, indulge in it! Really experience the gratitude, and keep in mind that this way of thinking will begin to improve your life. More and more, you will see positive events being attracted to you every day.

Chapter 5

The Law of Attraction and Friends

A friend is one of the nicest things you can have,
and one of the best things you can be.

Douglas Pagels

Who doesn't want more friends? The question is: What is the fastest and easiest way to obtain new friends? Well, by *attracting* them. A friend is someone who is *attracted* to you so much that they would title your relationship as "friends." If you have the ability to communicate, you have the ability to have friendships.

Positive Friendship Vibrations

The first step to acquiring more companions is appreciating the friends you already have. Focus on everything they have done for you and how many experiences you have shared together. Without them, what part of you would be missing right now?

After you really feel the appreciation of your current friends, begin to think about what types of new friends you would like. Do you want friends who are interested in video games? How about friends who like to play guitar, or friends who enjoy fashion? It is up to you to decide what type of "crew" you would like.

If you haven't realized it yet, this Law of Attraction stuff is all about confidence and the belief that you can, in fact, achieve what you truly want.

If everyone in this world actually believed they could obtain the things they want, there would never be someone with a desire unfulfilled, and that includes the desire for wonderful friendships.

But be completely aware when attracting your new friends. Make sure to focus *only* on the positive points of your ideal friends. Mixed feelings and emotions can make a huge difference in what and who you are attracting.

How Josh Attracted a New "Friend"

Josh: Age 14, 9th Grade

My buddy, Josh, was the kind of kid who had a few friends he'd had his whole life, but who never seemed to develop new friendships. After I explained to him about how the Law of Attraction works in attracting friends, he began to picture friends who were interested in *Lord of the Rings*, played video games, and loved computers. So, like the law always does, it matched his thoughts and vibrations. Within a week, he told me he had already found a new friend with the same interests as him. Success, right? Well, sort of. Josh's new friend was interested in the subjects Josh had visualized, but he was also basically addicted to video games and never had time to hang out! I had to explain why he attracted this into his life. Josh wasn't thinking of a friend who actually wanted to hang out and have a good time. He simply desired a friend with the same interests as him. He needed to be more specific about the kind of friend he wanted to attract. That is why I say be aware, and make it completely clear to yourself what type of friends you want; don't stop at a simple description.

The Issue with "Best Friends"

When I was younger, something made me different from other kids and still does today: I never had a best friend. I had some really good friends, but I never called someone my best friend. Want to know why?

Calling someone or something the "best" limits your possibilities dramatically. If you already *have* a "best" friend, in your subconscious mind, then no one else can be a better friend. So, in that case, you're unable to attract more friends with the same or better qualities as your "best" friend. Why would you want that?

Therefore, I decided to attract a *group* of "best" friends. I never called any single friend my best friend. When people would ask, "Who's your best friend, Chris?" I would simply say, "All my friends are." Truthfully, they all were, because the mindset and the vibes I put off attracted all of the best people I could have as friends at the time.

Why have one best friend when you can have ten? This applies to any situation in your life where you use the word "best." Saying things like "Last school year was the best!" or "This job is the best," or "That teacher was the best!" or "Tenth grade summer was the best!" restricts your opportunities to create something even better. "Best" is a limiting word, so remove it from your vocabulary! Replace it with words such as "wonderful," "fantastic," "brilliant," and "great." You can even say "one of the best" or "the best SO far."

So what type of friends would you like? I have made a sample worksheet that will help you to attract your ideal friends.

My Friendship Quality Attraction List

My Ideal Friends…

1. Accept me for who I am.

2. Can hold long conversations.

3. Love to hang out and have fun.

4. Are willing to learn about the Law of Attraction.

5. Listen to rock music.

6. *You can fill in the rest…*

7.

8.

9.

10.

Performing this exercise, and deliberately viewing it every day, will guarantee progress in your friendship situation. I have seen many teens use this simple list, and within a short period of time, they began meeting the friends they truly desired.

If you do not know what your ideal friendship qualities are, you can use step one of the three-step process to find out. By writing down what you don't want in a friend, it will become clear what you do want.

Now, I'm not saying that if you use Law of Attraction exercises, people will randomly walk up to you and shout, "Want to be friends?!" Some might (anything's possible!), but most will require your active effort.

That is why it is not very likely that you can sit in your driveway hoping for a Lamborghini and, within a few days, watch it magically pull up. The Law of Attraction will attract situations, ideas, and opportunities for you to *take action*. Some people misunderstand the law as an express delivery service. But while they're waiting for an overnight delivery, the "true attractors" are out in the real world making things happen. The next chapter will explain how you can add action to your thoughts, emotions, and vibrations to achieve the best possible results.

Chapter 6

Ten Ways to Speed Up
Your Manifesting

*The simplest way for me to look at
the Law of Attraction
is if I think of myself as a magnet,
and I know a magnet will attract to it.*

John Assaraf

Christopher A. Combates

As I mentioned in the previous chapter, in order for the Law of Attraction to work, our thoughts must be accompanied by positive action. In most cases, the more action you put into it, the faster your desires show up. Here are ten action steps that I have found to be particularly effective in my life.

1. Create a Vision Box or Vision Board

A vision box/vision board is a fun and interesting way to increase your manifesting speed. It displays your true desires and allows you to see them in a physical form.

In order to create one, you must first find a container or board. The type of container doesn't matter; it can be a shoebox or a wooden chest you made in shop class. If you would rather have a board to hang up, a white or cork board works best. After choosing your ideal container or board, label it "Vision ____." Now the magic begins. Print out pictures of your desires from the Internet, or simply skim magazines and cut out images that relate to your desires. Actual objects can be used as well, although it might be challenging to put an object on a flat board.

Each time you place something in or on your vision tool, the vibration of hope and desire is increased. From that point on, your subconscious mind remembers that action and steadily increases your vibration. You can glance at your vision tool whenever you want. While doing so, really feel the emotions that the images and objects create. Doing this will increase your manifesting speed tremendously.

2. Make a Goal Card

Goal cards are very popular throughout the world, in all aspects of goal-setting and achieving. They are an awesome way to increase manifestation speed because you are reminded constantly of your goal/desire. The first step to making a card is to identify your most important goal. It can be big or small, life changing or simple. A quick and easy method of doing this was created by self-help expert, Brian Tracy. In his technique, you write down ten goals you would like to achieve in a year. Some examples would be:

- All As and Bs on my report card
- Buy my first car
- Save $1,500
- Find a girlfriend/boyfriend

After you write down ten goals, select one that would have the most positive impact on your life if you achieved it in one day. Usually, the answer will pop out at you. Circle it; this is the goal that will go on your card. In order to manifest faster, you must carry this card with you at all times. Glance at it whenever you have the chance. Feel the emotions of having or acquiring your goal. Here's an example of a Goal Card:

<u>My Goal</u>: An Awesome, Impressive Report Card

<u>Detailed</u>: I Will Receive an Awesome, Impressive Report Card Every Semester for the Rest of the School Year.

<u>Exact</u>: As and Bs in Every Class.

<u>What to Do</u>: Pay Full Attention in Class and Always Ask Questions. Complete All Assignments on Time, Including

Homework. Stay for Extra Help if Needed.

You can copy the format of the card above or create one on your own. Personally, I like to laminate my goal cards. It only costs about a dollar, and it will last a lot longer than normal paper. These cards make a huge impact on the manifestation speed of your desire. The first one I made was about my goal of writing this book. Look where it got me!

3. Write Down an Appreciation List

As stated earlier, gratitude is one of the strongest positive emotions. When you begin to live in an "attitude of gratitude," the positives will start flying at you. If you want more of something, simply feel as much gratitude as possible for that specific thing. **The more gratitude you have, the stronger your vibration; the stronger your vibration, the faster you will manifest.**

Creating an appreciation list and actively adding to it every day will dramatically increase your positive vibes. It is very easy and quick to do. Take a piece of paper and write "Appreciation List" at the top. Put the date under the title, and write under the date, "Today I am thankful for…" You can write down as many entries as you want—the more the better!

The most important thing to remember is to really feel the emotion of gratitude while doing this exercise. Anyone can sit in his or her room and repeat bland lines over and over. But without the true feeling, this list will not be useful. While reading and writing your list, imagine how you would feel if you didn't have all the things you wrote down. That will spark some realization of how grateful you *should* be. Following is an Appreciation List that I wrote:

Appreciation List

Today, I am thankful for...

- Waking up in a comfortable bed
- The hot water in my shower
- All the clothes that I have
- A "free" ride to school
- All of my friends in school
- The food that I ate at lunch (even if it's not the best-tasting food in the world...)
- The education that I am NOT paying for
- This book!
- My family
- Being alive!

4. Put a Symbol Chart on Your Ceiling

When I first discovered the Law of Attraction, I needed a way to express my desires. I hadn't yet read about any tools or methods of doing this, so I decided to make my own. Thus, the symbol chart was created.

A symbol chart is simply a piece of paper with symbols drawn on it. Every image represents something you desire, whether you already have it or not. Ideally, this should be placed on your ceiling above your bed so that you can review every symbol before you go to sleep. After looking at each one, visualize yourself obtaining and having whatever the symbol represents. The idea is to get in the vibration that matches your desires. This is an awesome and creative way to do it.

Following are a few illustrations of my personal symbols and their meanings. You can copy my examples, or you can form your own. Whatever you do, make sure to review your chart every night.

Excellent health

 Plenty of money

 Abundance of love

 Remarkable grades

 Happiness in general

5. Keep an Evidence Journal

When you first begin using the Law of Attraction, you will most likely have some doubts. I had quite a bit, and most of my friends did, too. Doubt is the main reason for slow manifestation, so the objective is to remove doubt and create belief. A useful way to go about this is with an evidence journal.

This journal is a lot different from any other. It is used to record occurrences of the Law of Attraction in your daily life. The more evidence and proof you see that the law is real, the more doubt will be removed and the faster you will manifest. Without belief, it is nearly impossible to manifest anything consciously. The human mind usually needs proof or evidence about something before it creates a belief. As soon as I began recording the proof happening all around me, positive situations, objects, and relationships seemed to adore me.

Following is a sample journal. Remember that anything can be evidence, from a small coincidence to a long-term achievement.

Evidence Journal Entry 4/20/09

-Today, I woke up with a song stuck in my head. It was stuck there all day. When I got out of school, that same song came on the radio!

-For a while now, I've been trying to avoid a certain person. She is really negative and annoying. It is hard not to think about it. When I went to the mall, the first person I ran into was her…

-Yesterday, I decided I needed a part-time job. I thought about where to work during school. Today, my friend walked up to me and asked if I wanted to work with him at a clothing store!

6. Talk About Your Desires with Friends

As you already know, attention, energy, and focus are the keys to manifesting. This can be made into a simple formula: A+E+F = MS. MS means Manifest Speed. If you are not the math type, simply remember that attention, energy, and focus are extremely important in this process.

A great way to apply A, E, and F is to talk about it! Words create massive amounts of attention to whatever they're directed toward. So, instead of chatting about negative topics with your friends, talk about what you want! Every negative word brings you farther away from your desires. So, go ahead and tell your friends what you want! Encourage them to express their desires as well. It will be an awesome change in your friendship, and you will be surprised at how much faster you reach your desires. An added benefit of talking about positive things with your friends is that it will bring you closer than ever. You will feel the emotions of excitement and joy together, rather than dread and fear. Negative emotions will only destroy your relationship in the long run. Talk about the positives, and you and your friends will succeed together!

7. Daydream About Your Desires

Growing up, many kids are told to stop daydreaming or to "get your head out of the clouds." This concept is completely wrong. Daydream about your desires whenever you get the chance! This will only bring you closer to them. (When I say "whenever you get the chance," I mean, of course, when you're not taking a test in school or driving a car. Common sense will tell you this is a bad decision.) Daydream if you finish your test early, or if you have some free time waiting for the bus. Simply waiting does not do you any good. Use the power of your brain, combined with the Law of Attraction, to bring your life into harmony with whatever you want!

When you are daydreaming, remember to visualize a clear, distinct image of your desires. The clearer you get, the faster you will manifest.

8. Study the Law of Attraction

The purpose of this book is to *introduce* you to the Law of Attraction. My intention is that this will be the first step in your quest for Law of Attraction knowledge. It would be in your best interest to continue reading about and studying the Law of Attraction after you finish this book.

The more methods and information you discover about this law, the faster you will manifest your larger desires. There is so much to learn and so many resources to learn it from—movies, videos, books, online—so find the sources that fit you the best.

Go out into the world and learn from the experts I learned from, including Michael Losier, Esther and Jerry Hicks, Bob Proctor, Marla Martenson, Napoleon Hill, and many more. I have provided a list of Suggested Resources at the end of this book. Go over them and choose those that resonate with you. The more you learn, the more you'll manifest.

9. Teach Your Friends and Family

Spread this information to anyone and everyone: family, friends, teachers, and siblings! The more you give, the more you will get. After reading this book, you will become the teacher! If someone you know is having any type of problem, mention the law. Explain to them that they hold the power to change their lives, however bad their situation. Hand them this awesome quote by Michael Losier on a piece of paper.

You don't always get what you want, but you always get what you vibrate.

Of course, it's important to remember that if someone didn't ask the question, they don't always want to hear the answer! As a general rule, most people will respond negatively to a person attempting to shove information at them. (Think of how you respond to your parents when they do this to you.) If you run up to your friend shouting, "The Law of Attraction! You need to learn it!" he or she will probably think you are crazy and reject what you have to say. This is the same reason that most telemarketers never make sales! They are considered annoying, and people aren't interested in what they have to say. This could happen to you if you try to force your knowledge of the Law of Attraction on your friends and family.

There are some strategies, though, that will interest your friends enough to start the ball rolling without being pushy or turning people off. One way to spark your friends' and family's interest in the Law of Attraction is to ask certain statements and questions. This method "secretly" generates a desire inside of them, without their even knowing it!

- Have you had a coincidence lately?
- I found a method of improving my life. I wish you knew about it!
- There's this awesome stuff I just read…

- If you ever have a problem, let me know. I found a technique that solved most of mine.
- Are you a lucky person?

With any one of these questions, you can begin a conversation that could change someone's life.

10. Be Happy!

Who doesn't want to be happy? Even if this Law of Attraction stuff wasn't real, why not be happy all the time? The fact that happiness increases your manifesting speed tremendously is just a bonus!

Many people ask, "How can I be happy when everyone around me isn't?" This is the main difference between successful people and what some call "losers." Successful people have control over their emotions, no matter the circumstances. It is a skill that can be developed. Learning to have control of your feelings will make your life a thousand times better. As said by the famous motivational speaker Les Brown:

If you can't be happy, what else is there?

The quote above is so true that it gives me the chills. When it comes down to it, everyone's goal is to be happy! Humans devolved the word "happiness" to describe how it feels when in a positive vibration. So the happier you are, the more desires you will manifest, and the faster they will come.

Chapter 7

A Final Word

Everything you want is out there waiting for you to ask.
Everything you want also wants you.
But you have to take action to get it.

Jack Canfield

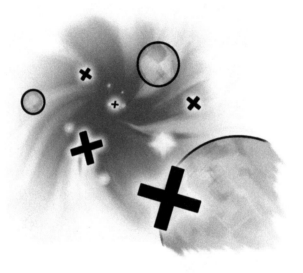

In many Law of Attraction books, a well-known four-step process is introduced in the early chapters. I have waited until now because I feel it is best to completely explain the Law of Attraction with many examples before the four-step process is introduced. Many people, after hearing about the Law of Attraction and trying to use it in their lives, proclaim, "The Law of Attraction didn't work for me." When you really look into it, though, you can see why. They follow the four-step process without really understanding the Law of Attraction beforehand. Because they haven't experienced the evidence of its truth, a ton of doubt is still inside of them, which then sets them up for failure. So now that you have learned the basics, I will give you this four-step process.

The Four Steps of the Law of Attraction

1. Know what you want.

If you have read this entire book, you will know that when I say "know what you want," this does not mean a general idea. You have to make it absolutely clear what you want; every detail and preference must be recognized. The more specific you are, the more you will manifest your true desires.

2. Ask for it.

Ask the universe for your desire. While you are asking, feel the intense aspiration that you have for this situation or item. The strength of your desire will affect the rate at which you manifest. People with a burning desire will manifest at a faster rate.

3. Feel the emotions of already having it.

This is a *very important* step in the process. When you feel the emotions of already having your item or situation, the Law of Attraction will check on your vibe, and match it with the situations and items that are on the same vibration!

4. Allow it into your life.

Many people who really want something never seem to get it. They say they have a burning desire, they ask for it, and even feel the emotions of already having it. The problem is that they never actually *believe* they can have or obtain it. This is where most people tend to have trouble. At first, allowing something into your life is not easy. Our mindsets have brainwashed us into thinking we can only have, be, or receive certain things, based on our circumstances. This is completely wrong and should be changed immediately after reading this page. Realize that no matter what your circumstances, anything you want with a strong enough desire, passion, and belief can be achieved. Look around. It happens all the time, and often to people who seemed to have no "realistic" hope of ever achieving their dreams.

Living Your Life Like the Sims!

If you have ever played the video game *The Sims*, you understand what I mean by "Living Your Life Like the Sims." If not, I will give you a short description of what I'm talking about.

The Sims video game gives you the opportunity to create your own life. You begin the game by designing every aspect of your character's life. Whether you are married or single, live in a shack or a mansion, it is all up to you. Whatever your "desire," a click of a button will bring it to you. This can be directly translated into real life, using the Law of Attraction. When it comes down to it, everyone is responsible for his or her own life. Think of the video game controller as your brain, and the design screen as your thoughts. If you live life in this way, nothing will seem impossible. You will begin to realize that you are accountable for your quality of life, not your circumstances.

You can begin to plan out your ideal life today, just like the Sims! Where do you want to live? What will your career be? What kind of car do you want to drive? These are all questions you should begin to ask yourself. Put these down on paper and review them every day. And remember, if you don't believe it is possible, then "it's impossible" is what you are attracting.

Whether you think you can or think you can't, either way you are right.

This quote by Henry Ford explains it all. If you don't believe you have the power to create your own life, you are right. If you believe you can create your ideal life, you are right. Which one sounds more enjoyable? Once again, it is up to you.

The common saying "Believe in yourself!" has more value than you think. When you begin to trust that your brain is life's controller, your life will take on new meaning. Faith and belief are key to benefiting from the Law of Attraction. Without them, this law will remain a myth. So why not try it out? What do you have to lose? Start believing today, and plan out your ideal life!

Acknowledgments

I want to give my deepest gratitude to the following people who made this book possible:

First and foremost, I would like to thank my family for their support, encouragement, and guidance. Even when times in our house were hard, your love and input helped me to stay motivated and keep going.

To Michael Losier, I never would have done this book without you. When I first started, I thought it would be a simple hobby, but you put me on track and revealed my true potential. You are an excellent mentor and friend. Thank you!

To Bettie Youngs, another wonderful mentor and the reason this book is in front of you. Many lessons of book writing and publishing were learned through the magic of you and Paul Burt as publishers of Teen Town Press. A special shout-out to developmental editor, Lynn Hess, and content editor, Susan Heim. You made my manuscript sing!

Last but far from least, a big thanks to my Facebook friends who supported me throughout this process, and to so many others whose encouraging comments and suggestions kept me driven to produce an awesome book! I am truly grateful and admire you all.

Suggested Resources

Books

- *Law of Attraction*, by Michael J. Losier (Wellness Central, 2007)
- *The Secret*, by Rhonda Byrne (Atria Books/Beyond Words, 2006)
- *Beyond the Secret,* by Lisa Love (Hampton Roads, 2007)
- *Think and Grow Rich,* by Napoleon Hill (Wilder Publications, 2008)
- *The Power of Your Subconscious Mind,* by Joseph Murphy (Martino Fine Books, 2009)
- *The Law of Attraction: The Basics of the Teachings of Abraham*, by Esther and Jerry Hicks (Hay House, 2006)
- *The Psychology of Winning,* by Denis Waitley (Berkley, 1986)
- *Excuse Me, Your Life Is Waiting,* by Lynn Grabhorn (Hampton Roads, 2003)
- *Excuse Me, Your Soul Mate Is Waiting,* by Marla Martenson (Hampton Roads, 2008)
- *You Were Born Rich*, by Bob Proctor (LifeSuccess Productions, 1997)
- *A Taste-Berry Teen's Guide to Setting and Achieving Goals*, by Jennifer Leigh Youngs (HCI Teens, 2002)
- *365 Days of Taste-Berry Inspiration for Teens,* by Jennifer Leigh Youngs (HCI Teens, 2003)

Movies/Video

- *The Secret* (2006)
- *What the Bleep Do We Know?* (2005)
- Michael Losier's YouTube Channel (ML3001)
- Esther and Jerry Hicks's YouTube Channel (AbrahamHicks)
- Sonia Ricotti's YouTube Channel (soniari)

About the Author

Christopher A. Combates is a sixteen-year-old self-help enthusiast, entrepreneur, and aspiring music artist. He has huge dreams for the future and believes in endless possibilities. He currently attends high school in New Jersey. The extreme diversity in his environment has sparked many of his creative ideas. Chris loves to meet many different types of people and collaborate with them. If you'd like to reach Chris with questions or business inquires, please contact him through his website at www.vibe-nation.com.

...books that inform and inspire

Visit our website at
www.TeenTownPress.com

CPSIA information can be obtained
at www.ICGtesting.com
Printed in the USA
FSHW012308301118

9 781936 332298